**Date: 4/14/21**

**J BIO BIDEN**
**Hansen, Grace,**
**Joe Biden /**

PALM BEACH COUNTY
LIBRARY SYSTEM
3650 SUMMIT BLVD.
WEST PALM BEACH, FL 33406

D1267132

# Joe Biden

by Grace Hansen

UNITED STATES PRESIDENT BIOGRAPHIES

Abdo Kids Jumbo is an Imprint of Abdo Kids
abdobooks.com

**abdobooks.com**

Published by Abdo Kids, a division of ABDO, P.O. Box 398166, Minneapolis, Minnesota 55439.
Copyright © 2021 by Abdo Consulting Group, Inc. International copyrights reserved in all countries.
No part of this book may be reproduced in any form without written permission from the publisher.
Abdo Kids Jumbo™ is a trademark and logo of Abdo Kids.

Printed in the United States of America, North Mankato, Minnesota.

102020

012021

THIS BOOK CONTAINS
RECYCLED MATERIALS

Photo Credits: Alamy, AP Images, Getty Images, iStock, Thinkstock, ©Shutterstock PREMIER p.Cover

Production Contributors: Teddy Borth, Jennie Forsberg, Grace Hansen
Design Contributors: Laura Mitchell, Dorothy Toth

Library of Congress Control Number: 2020940252

Publisher's Cataloging-in-Publication Data

Names: Hansen, Grace, author.

Title: Joe Biden / by Grace Hansen

Description: Minneapolis, Minnesota : Abdo Kids, 2021 | Series: United States president biographies |
    Includes online resources and index.

Identifiers: ISBN 9781098206932 (lib. bdg.) | ISBN 9781098206956 (ebook) | ISBN 9781098206963
    (Read-to-Me ebook)

Subjects: LCSH: Biden, Joseph R., Jr.--Juvenile literature. | Vice-Presidents--United States--Biography--
    Juvenile literature. | Presidents--United States--Biography--Juvenile literature. | Legislators--United
    States--Biography--Juvenile literature.

Classification: DDC 973.93--dc23

# Table of Contents

## Early Years

Joseph Robinette Biden, Jr. was born in Scranton, Pennsylvania, on November 20, 1942. The Biden family moved to Claymont, Delaware, when Joe was 10.

Scranton, Pennsylvania

Delaware

Pennsylvania

5

## Education

Joe was known as a natural leader among his classmates. He was a star on the football team in high school. He was also voted **class president** his junior and senior years.

1961

**Archmere Academy
college preparatory school**

7

Joe attended college at the University of Delaware. He graduated in history and **political science** in 1965. He went on to study law at Syracuse University in Syracuse, New York.

1965

University of Delaware

9

## Family & Tragedy

Biden and Neilia Hunter met at Syracuse. They married in 1966 and had three children together. In 1972, Neilia was in a tragic car accident. Neilia and Naomi, the couple's daughter, did not survive.

## US Capitol to the White House

Just before the accident, Biden won a Delaware seat in the US Senate. Many did not think he would win. But Biden had run a tireless campaign.

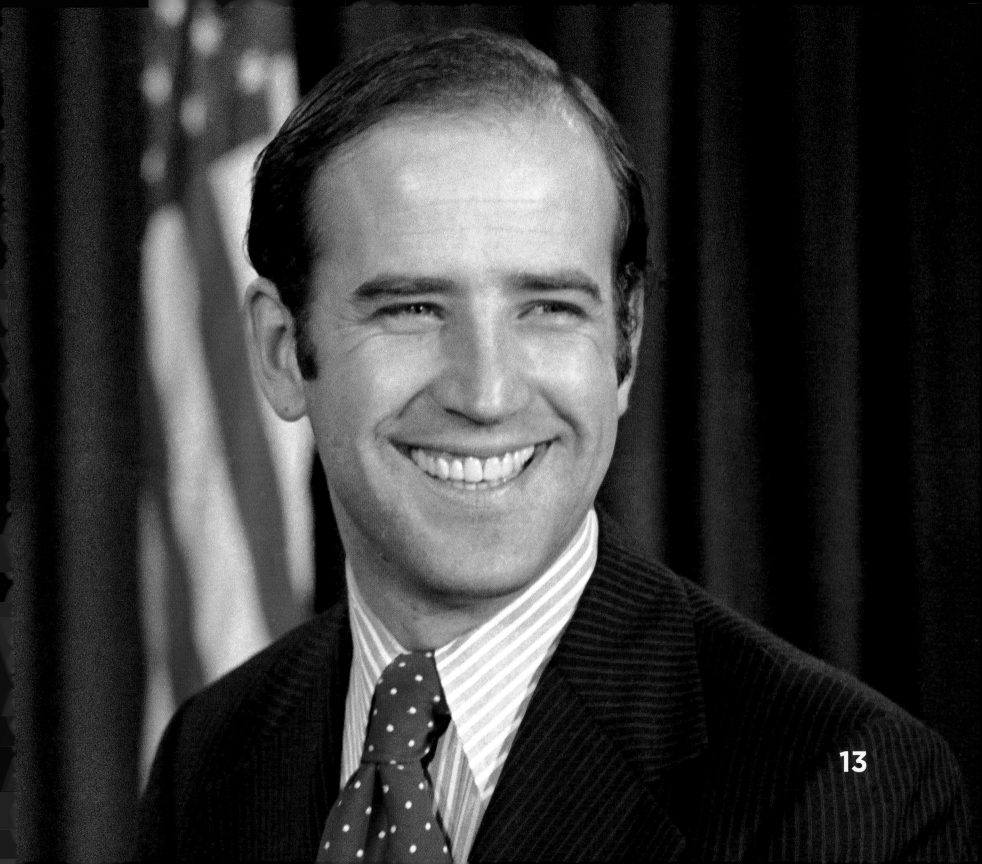

13

Biden served in the Senate until he was offered a new job. Presidential hopeful Barack Obama asked Biden to be his running mate. Obama won the election. He was sworn in on January 20, 2009. That day, Biden became vice president of the United States.

15

President Obama was reelected in 2012. Biden served another term as VP. On January 12, 2017, Obama honored Biden with the Presidential Medal of Freedom with **distinction**. Obama said it was for Biden's lifetime of service and love of country.

Biden announced in April 2019 that he would run for president. In August 2020, Biden became the official Democratic presidential **nominee**. He asked Kamala Harris to be his running mate.

The 2020 presidential election was different due to the COVID-19 pandemic. Many of Biden's political events were done virtually. But the unique **campaign** and efforts paid off. Joe Biden was elected the 46th president of the United States!

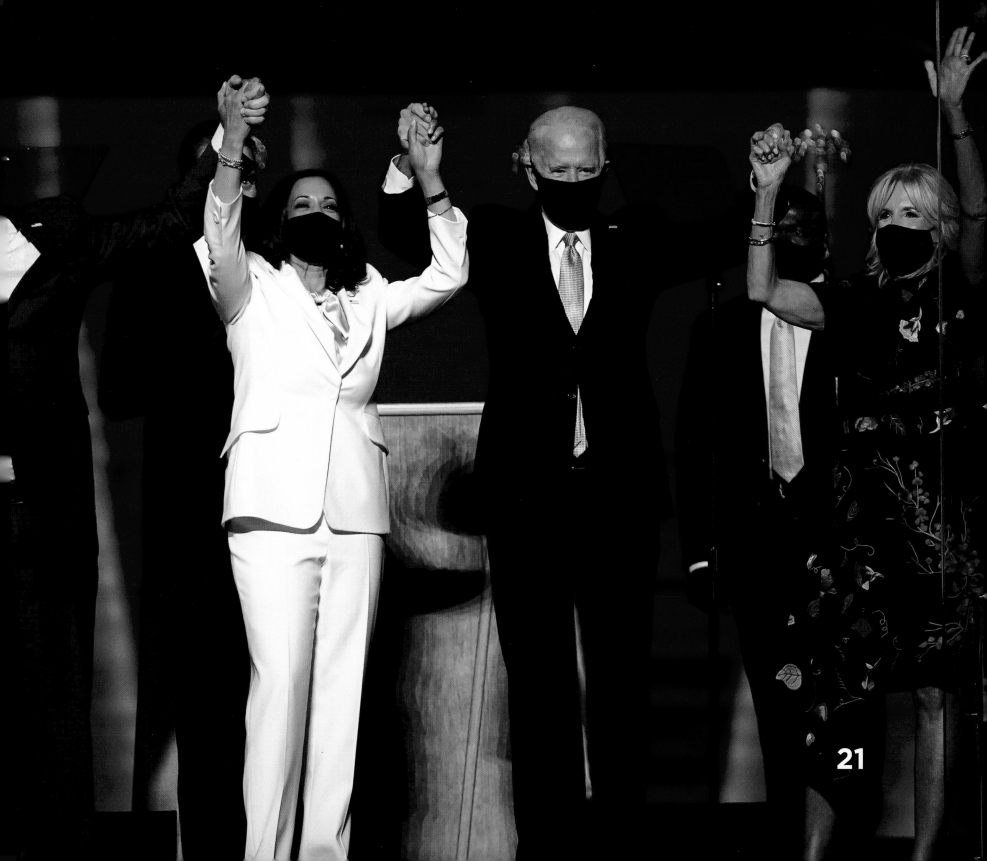

21

# More Facts

- When Biden ran for **US Senate**, he had very little money to **campaign** with. His family, including his sister and parents, helped Joe go door-to-door to meet voters.

- Biden earned the nickname Amtrak Joe during his time in the Senate. He wanted his sons' lives to stay as normal as possible. He traveled 120 miles (193 km) on the Amtrak train every day.

- Joe Biden married his second wife Jill in 1977. They had a daughter, Ashley, in 1980. Jill helped raise Joe and Neilia's sons, Hunter and Beau.

# Glossary

**campaign** – a series of actions carried out in order to reach a particular goal. In politics, the goal is to win an election.

**class president** – an elected leader of a student body class and the head of a student council.

**distinction** – with special recognition or excellence.

**nominee** – a person or thing that has been nominated for an office or honor.

**political science** – the science of politics, political institutions, and the principles and methods of government.

**US Senate** – one of the two houses of the United States Congress. The Senate is made up of senators, each representing a single state. The Senate has several powers in US government.

23

# Index

**Abdo Kids ONLINE**
FREE! ONLINE MULTIMEDIA RESOURCES

Visit **abdokids.com** to access crafts, games, videos, and more!

Use Abdo Kids code

**UJK6932**

or scan this QR code!